Solitaire

by Rosary Hartel O'Neill

A Samuel French Acting Edition

New York Hollywood London Toronto

SAMUELFRENCH.COM

Copyright © 2008, 2010 by Rosary Hartel O'Neill
ALL RIGHTS RESERVED

CAUTION: Professionals and amateurs are hereby warned that *SOLITAIRE* is subject to a licensing fee. It is fully protected under the copyright laws of the United States of America, the British Commonwealth, including Canada, and all other countries of the Copyright Union. All rights, including professional, amateur, motion picture, recitation, lecturing, public reading, radio broadcasting, television and the rights of translation into foreign languages are strictly reserved. In its present form the play is dedicated to the reading public only.

The amateur and professional live stage performance rights to *SOLITAIRE* are controlled exclusively by Samuel French, Inc., and licensing arrangements and performance licenses must be secured well in advance of presentation. PLEASE NOTE that amateur licensing fees are set upon application in accordance with your producing circumstances. When applying for a licensing quotation and a performance license please give us the number of performances intended, dates of production, your seating capacity and admission fee. Licensing fees are payable one week before the opening performance of the play to Samuel French, Inc., at 45 W. 25th Street, New York, NY 10010.

Licensing fee of the required amount must be paid whether the play is presented for charity or gain and whether or not admission is charged.

Professional/Stock licensing fees quoted upon application to Samuel French, Inc.

For all other rights than those stipulated above, apply to: The Marton Agency, 1 Union Square West, Suite 815, New York, NY 10003; Info@MartonAgency.com.

Particular emphasis is laid on the question of amateur or professional readings, permission and terms for which must be secured in writing from Samuel French, Inc.

Copying from this book in whole or in part is strictly forbidden by law, and the right of performance is not transferable.

Whenever the play is produced the following notice must appear on all programs, printing and advertising for the play: "Produced by special arrangement with Samuel French, Inc."

Due authorship credit must be given on all programs, printing and advertising for the play.

ISBN 978-0-573-69790-6   Printed in U.S.A.   #29254

No one shall commit or authorize any act or omission by which the copyright of, or the right to copyright, this play may be impaired.

No one shall make any changes in this play for the purpose of production.

Publication of this play does not imply availability for performance. Both amateurs and professionals considering a production are strongly advised in their own interests to apply to Samuel French, Inc., for written permission before starting rehearsals, advertising, or booking a theatre.

No part of this book may be reproduced, stored in a retrieval system, or transmitted in any form, by any means, now known or yet to be invented, including mechanical, electronic, photocopying, recording, videotaping, or otherwise, without the prior written permission of the publisher.

MUSIC USE NOTE

Licensees are solely responsible for obtaining formal written permission from copyright owners to use copyrighted music in the performance of this play and are strongly cautioned to do so. If no such permission is obtained by the licensee, then the licensee must use only original music that the licensee owns and controls. Licensees are solely responsible and liable for all music clearances and shall indemnify the copyright owners of the play and their licensing agent, Samuel French, Inc., against any costs, expenses, losses and liabilities arising from the use of music by licensees.

IMPORTANT BILLING AND CREDIT REQUIREMENTS

All producers of *SOLITAIRE must* give credit to the Author of the Play in all programs distributed in connection with performances of the Play, and in all instances in which the title of the Play appears for the purposes of advertising, publicizing or otherwise exploiting the Play and/or a production. The name of the Author *must* appear on a separate line on which no other name appears, immediately following the title and *must* appear in size of type not less than fifty percent of the size of the title type.

CHARACTERS

IRENE DUBONNET (MIMI) – 60+. Strong, stylish widow of one month. Wears a hat cocked over one eye, a neck smothered with pearls, a 5-caret solitaire. Irene dresses young—dying her hair a richer version of red to offset her violet eyes—and flashing a fan, color coordinated to each outfit, against the heat. Irene could pass for forty.

ROOSTER DUBONNET (ROO) – 30. Her son, an artist and a dreamer with the boyish charm of a college freshman. Very careless. Rooster appears pale, sickly, with flushed cheeks and locks of hair tumbling in disarray over his forehead. An uncertainty is at the center of all his choices. Rooster forgets to change his clothes.

QUINT LEGERE – 45. Irene's son-in-law, a driven accountant. Very neat. No matter what Quint wears, his broad shoulders and smooth tan make him look first class. Quint changes his shirt four times a day to keep crisp in the summer. Quint feels it's important to dress your best when you feel your worst.

BUNKY – 20. The only son of Quint and ex-wife Kitten Dubonnet Legere. Nonchalant and seductive in blue jeans and boots, he refuses to relate to school. He wears a tee-shirt which reads, "Protect Wild Life. Throw a Party." Bunky is a rebel—with a wild streak of fun. He quells his passion for adventure by absorbing himself in blues music and busywork for his relatives.

JASMINE RUSH – 36. Adopted daughter of Irene Dubonnet, glamorous actress. Dresses outrageously—over the edge of Italian fashion—with heavy eye make-up and ensembles contoured to her body and legs. The most famous hand model in the world, Jasmine needs help doing ordinary things like opening bottles, zipping gowns, dialing the phone—so she won't rip a nail.

TIME

The not-too-distant present. July 4th weekend.

SETTING

Gallery of "Serenity," a summer mansion, Pass Christian, Mississippi.

Act One: Scene one. "Serenity." Sunday, July third. Late afternoon.

Scene two. "Serenity." The next day. Twilight.

Act Two: "Serenity." Sunday afternoon, one week later.

SOLITAIRE was first performed in November 1993 at the American Center, Paris..

SOLITAIRE

ACT ONE

Scene One

(The gallery of a Greek Revival home facing the Gulf of Mexico. Pass Christian, Mississippi. The Gulf Coast is the haunt of wealthy but weary New Orleanians: people wearing seersucker suits and white sundresses, people who might otherwise dine at Antoine's Restaurant in New Orleans. The mansion (one of the few intact after Hurricane Camille) reminds one of plantation culture, of that doomed if circumspect way of life.

The gallery overlooks a paradise of flowers and veil after veil of shrubbery, a pool, a duck pond, gardens with birds, marshes and woods. Dubbed "Serenity," the estate remains the heart of a kingdom of wildlife, their final refuge from a world grown too strange, too hard, and too disturbing.

The action passes on a gallery, with baskets of blue hydrangeas and colored garden furniture placed over soft brick. A rotating ceiling fan is spinning shadows overhead. Windows catch reflections from the trees and moss, their shutters, perfect for eavesdropping, trembling ever so slightly. The sturdy columns of plastered brick evoke nostalgia while appearing lost in space. They seem to ascend into the sky. The place has a haunted elegant quality, as if it had been constructed for a reception after a defeat. The ghost of old fears, the gallery fuses light and shadow in the unrelenting heat. Today, the gallery feels luminous, public, and safe, i.e., conducive to mindless chatter.

A lazy Sunday tableau. A tray of scotch and bourbon, a bucket of ice, and hors d'oeuvres: olives, celery, pickles, caviar, and cheese straws are set out for Sunday cocktails.)

(SOUND: *Throughout the act, there are heard the soft cries of sea gulls and the lapping of waves. Something like Jacques Brel music resounds.)*

(LIGHTS: *A surreal light fades up on* **IRENE DUBONNET** *playing Solitaire.)*

(As **IRENE** *speaks, silhouettes of the other characters stroll through the scene as if she is calling up memories.)*

IRENE. I belong to a part of society rarely viewed by outsiders— the Southern top drawer. We're the handful of families who live on and above the rest. East Coast boarding schools and junior year abroad. Mint juleps and Russian caviar. We slip inside a private door at Antoine's Restaurant and phone for our personal waiter to escort us to a back room. We are the people the great Louisiana hotels were built for—the lobbies showcasing the Mississippi River, the silver service *(cont.)* steaming with jasmine tea, the harpist strumming the "Clair de Lune." Our women have been plumed and manicured, and our men steeled to position themselves for the slightest financial advantage. White suits in summer. Navy blazers for fall...a nurse to sleek down every wisp of hair, we dress exquisitely. No white shoes before May. No straw after July. Patent leather always a second choice. Taste is so inbred that we are impulsively stylish. My family is, I suspect, the most miserable one I know.

(**IRENE** *slams down the cards. Black out. All the characters exit.*)

SOLITAIRE

Scene Two

(German shepherds growl outside, hurling the scene into reality. **ROOSTER** *is in a rumpled white suit, loafers without socks.* **QUINT** *enters in smart business clothes.)*

QUINT. Tie up your dog, why don't you, Roo! Good-for-nothing guard dogs... won't let you in your own house! *(Wipes off the cuffs of his slacks)* Will you look at these pants!

BUNKY. Dad! Uncle Roo pulled another all-nighter!

ROOSTER. I watched the sun rise from Hancock Hospital emergency room.

QUINT. Too much partying!

ROOSTER. An overdose of pleasure. My lady love slipped and broke her toe.

BUNKY. What's that on your leg?

ROOSTER. A spider bite.

BUNKY. A black widow?

ROOSTER. No. An ordinary brown recluse.

QUINT. That's not the cancer returning.

BUNKY. You had cancer?

ROOSTER. A little melanoma. On the side of my nose. And on my neck.

BUNKY. What does it look like? Maybe I have it.

ROOSTER. Please! *(Wafting a mushroom)* Look! A mango-colored marvel from that landfill out back!

QUINT. Don't discuss the rear property.

ROOSTER. Only thing that catches your eye-

QUINT. Why do you walk back there when you get these reactions?

ROOSTER. I'm a hedonist living for pleasure in a state of disadvantage. Polyester, soap, dust! I'm allergic to practically everything!

QUINT. I love Mississippi! If I had $50, I'd buy it!

(SOUND: The phone rings. **QUINT** *grabs it and hangs up. It rings again.)*

*(***QUINT** *pours a scotch and water.* **ROOSTER** *peers through some binoculars.)*

ROOSTER. Things on the beach aren't what they seem. A patch of sand is scurrying away. Silver mackerel are flipping on the shore. Their habitat's vanishing!

QUINT. No one gets the Sunday paper here?

ROOSTER. My life's evaporating, too. I've no cash flow, and no credibility.

QUINT. Cash flow has nothing to do with credibility! Ha! You've no financial credibility as a part-time illustrator.

ROOSTER. I'm an artist.

QUINT. *(Picks up a book from Tulane University)* A law school catalog?

ROOSTER. I thought maybe I'd study criminal law. I need to find something with meaning.

QUINT. Criminal law? Do you want to wash your hands after shaking your clients' hands?

ROOSTER. *(Pouring a drink)* I'm almost thirty, and I've never had a job that could support me. *(Gestures to a wing of the house)* I open the icebox in my quarters, and see my reflection in the rear wall...Maybe I should get a master's degree in social work.

QUINT. Your Mama's property is worth a thousand dollars a square foot!

ROOSTER. I live high on the hog at Mama's but on my own...I'm just a scavenger sniffing around for loot!

QUINT. Take the nipple out of your mouth.

(SOUND: The phone rings. **QUINT** *answers it and changes his voice.)*

QUINT. No, Quint isn't here...call back after five...No, I can't take a message.

*(***QUINT** *bangs down the phone.)*

ROOSTER. Are you upset about something, Quint? You're the closest thing to a brother I've got.

QUINT. Brother-in-law.

ROOSTER. What's the difference?

QUINT. In-laws ain't family. Rules are different for in-laws than for family members.

(SOUND: The Our Lady Star of the Sea Church bells resound.)

*(***BUNKY** *dances in wearing a Mexican shirt. He shakes Mexican jumping beans.)*

BUNKY. *Buen-os Dios! Sino-ritas! Donde es los sombreros, piñatas!* Hey, Uncle Roo. These Mexican jumping beans are alive. Uncle Roo and I want to start our own gallery business.

ROOSTER. Now that the will's in probate, no one's supposed to ask Mama for money. I hope the lawyers will rush things.

QUINT. Your Mama has the lawyers paralyzed. Your old man had safe deposit boxes in every bank, up and down the Mississippi. Now she's bombarding the lawyers with conflicting information. You'll have to wait in line like the rest of us...for her to parcel out the estate.

BUNKY. Want a pickle?

*(***BUNKY** *pops an olive and nervously wipes his hand on his t-shirt. He exits)*

QUINT. Your mother is a power, a Cro-Magnon, Roo. You hit her with a crowbar, it don't make a dent.

ROOSTER. She bought a house for you and your wife.

QUINT. Ex-wife. Your mother has my best interest at heart except when it conflicts with her own.

ROOSTER. Bunky's still her only grandchild.

QUINT. Thank God I had a son. Look, this family's a circus! I've learned to jump through an increasingly difficult series of smaller and smaller flaming hoops. There's a world of private decisions being made around your dad's properties. Your mother and her advisors are inside the monastery, and we're out here in the bar.

ROOSTER. You're her accountant.

QUINT. She's hired a front man to frame me.

ROOSTER. Not Mama.

QUINT. A third-rate attorney, but a blood relative, her second cousin once removed.

ROOSTER. Clovis DeBango?

QUINT. He's a merger and acquisitions guy. He buys and sells people. Clovis's caught me before and he's going to get me big now.

ROOSTER. What did you do?

QUINT. I took out a note against the family insurance policy. I'm vice-president.

ROOSTER. You stole money!

QUINT. It's a paper deal. The account was flush.

ROOSTER. It wasn't your money.

QUINT. DeBango's frozen all my accounts. He's going to shut my firm down and send me to jail. DeBango's setting me up to be the fall guy for these dishonest family partnerships. The man's a gold-digger. He'd take a ring off a dead man's finger.

ROOSTER. What's DeBango's motive?

SOLITAIRE

QUINT. Do I want to analyze Frankenstein?

ROOSTER. Mama never hurt you.

QUINT. One person can do tremendous violence to another within the confines of a "happy" home. I saw a tomb with a sign on it, "I told you, I had high blood pressure."...Talk to your mother?

ROOSTER. I don't know how. Our conversations start happy and become more and more tragic.

QUINT. Just like life...I gave you a job in my CPA office.

ROOSTER. So I owe you?

QUINT. I'm trying to be as decent as possible in an indecent situation. My creditors are clobbering my brains out. Your dad was giving me his rear property for a wildlife refuge. I went in hock to grab all the adjacent land, but he kicked the bucket! Your mama pulled out.

QUINT. I hoped you'd find the steel in your back—to ramrod things and take control.

(BUNKY enters and hands QUINT a Federal Express envelope.)

QUINT. *(Seizes another drink)* Thanks.

BUNKY. Booze, so early!

QUINT. Just bracing myself for the lawyers. *(Perusing papers from the envelope)* I've been vaporized! That's corporate slang for terminated!

BUNKY. You're so calm about it.

QUINT. I feel a certain triumph that I won control over my emotions. That for now I can keep them at bay. *(Reviewing the envelope)* This is the real fear in life—being framed by your family, persons of integrity, with your interests at heart—not losers. The scent of money draws them out. The corpse is barely cold, but the kin approach, in packs, like mice. Each one squealing for a bite.

BUNKY. Sssh! Grandma'll be home from church soon.

QUINT. Let's not rile her up. We can upset Dad, though! Clovis DeBango hurls me this dart—this lethal document. *(Tosses an envelope at* **BUNKY***)* Tiny print destined to destroy. We're in Louisiana, redneck country. There are more lawyers licking their chops off bankruptcies here...than rats.

*(***ROOSTER** *puts an ice pack over his eyes and stretches out on the couch.)*

ROOSTER. I don't want to get in the middle of this.

QUINT. Tell your mother to call off DeBango. Lend me fifty thousand dollars. This is not some typhoon that's wiping out South America. I'm your brother-in-law.

ROOSTER. I don't feel good.

QUINT. If your mother thinks you're on my side, she'll help me out.

ROOSTER. I think I'm coming down with the flu.

QUINT. Talk to her. If not, I lose everything: the house, Bunky's education...

ROOSTER. Don't take this the wrong way, but nobody in the family trusts you. You lap up the booze. I'm sorry.

QUINT. Go on. You slit open the wound, dig your finger in it.

ROOSTER. Mama says you have a credibility gap downtown. Important people refuse to work with you.

QUINT. I'm telling y'all my neck's on the chopping block, and you're lifting the blade. They got the Mafia after me. Those guys compete in violence. Their currency is blood. They don't get their money, they'll hang my head on the gate.

ROOSTER. My advice to you, Quint, is to be a bit patient. She's an old woman... you'll outlast her.

QUINT. You're living off her and advising detachment. That's good.

ROOSTER. You asked for help.

QUINT. I asked you to do something.

ROOSTER. I'm an artist, you're the businessman.

QUINT. You're not going to weaken your position to help me. I see. You're an artist, so you can't think. You can't play politics. You can't zip your pants.

ROOSTER. I don't know how to say this, but I've been promoting DeBango. I recommended they remove your name from all family documents, and we slip you some money.

QUINT. *(Shocked, gasps for wind)* The...most...unsuspecting people...are turncoats.

ROOSTER. DeBango says that you keep having "credibility gaps."

QUINT. "Credibility gaps."

ROOSTER. Quint! We're saving the family land...for Bunky.

QUINT. DeBango's set up an irreversible trust to lock me out!

ROOSTER. That paper's a formality.

QUINT. You never had to hustle.

ROOSTER. Mama'll give it all back to you, Quint!

QUINT. You lie around here whining...like a weasel in heat.

*(***QUINT*** seizes an umbrella and swings at* **ROOSTER***)*

BUNKY. Dad, he's sick!

QUINT. Not too sick to think of his own interests. Decapitation is too good.

ROOSTER. Just rave away!

QUINT. This family has shut its doors on the murder of my career. They think my failure is beneath them.

BUNKY. *(Restraining* **QUINT***)* Roo just wanted to help me.

QUINT. Y'all can't deny my pain as if you could silence it beneath a river of booze.

ROOSTER. It's Mama's money.

QUINT. We were in a partnership. But it was never enough for her because she couldn't control me. *(Swigs a drink and imitates* **IRENE***)* "Don't worry, Quint. I'll help you if you get desperate. You can live in Clarence's room out back and repair the villa."

ROOSTER. Mama's losing her faculties one by one. Sometimes I'm the only person she confides in all week.

QUINT. Tell her to make a friend. What's missing is compassion for the individuals and issues involved and a set of standards for the restoration of decency. It's my fault that I trusted this family. A warning light should flash on whenever y'all approach. *(***QUINT** *exits)*

ROOSTER. So much has changed since I was a boy. Maybe I've changed. I'm surrounded by memories that have led me astray. I don't believe life's real. It's an illusion, so it doesn't bother me. If I thought it was real, I'd kill myself.

BUNKY. You promised to buy fireworks for the Fourth of July!

ROOSTER. I've got those catfish sketches to draw.

BUNKY. For that science textbook? Forget it! Dad's mad at Grandma. No one can tell her off because they want her money. And she's old.

ROOSTER. Cruelty doesn't come with age. All old people don't act like that. They eat their young here.

*(**SOUND**: Dogs bark offstage.)*

*(***IRENE** *enters.)*

IRENE. Quint! Roo! Tie up your dogs! Dogs mating on the lawn. Why can't Quint get a male dog or keep his dog in the pen?

ROOSTER. All right, Mama! *(Exits)*

BUNKY. Welcome home, Mimi!

IRENE. Bunky, get that.

BUNKY. Do I have to?

IRENE. Father Fannen focused his sermon today on money. He looked at the congregation and said: "Probably none of you have ever seen real pearls." Of course, it was the one day I wore mine to Star of the Sea. Undo these pearls, Roo. Father Fannen announced my age in Daddy's obituary in the church bulletin. He wants me to bequeath these pearls to Star of the Sea.

ROOSTER. Those real pearls you were willing me.

IRENE. After Mass, I managed to keep my graciousness and my distance simultaneously. I've never worn fake jewelry a day in my life.

ROOSTER. Irish priests may force you to change your ways.

IRENE. Ruthy May! *(Yanks off her pearls and places them on the table. Calling.)* That maid is probably lying lengthwise across the bed with my portable phone.

(SOUND: The phone rings. IRENE grabs it.)

IRENE. *(Into the phone)* Hello. Who?...It's for Quint. *(To QUINT)* Aren't you going to say, "Good morning"?

QUINT. Good morning.

IRENE. I hope you didn't ruin my Cadillac hauling your speed boat. Well, aren't you going to say, "Thanks"?

QUINT. Thanks. *(Into the phone)* Unifirst Bank for Savings went belly up! *(Flattens his hair back from his forehead)* No! *(QUINT dials another number and crosses upstage)*

IRENE. Roo, I want to update y'all all on that bill to preserve Mississippi wildlife.

QUINT. One minute! *(Exits)*

IRENE. I hope you're not tying up my phone. To continue with my story, the agent for the Department of the Interior and Forest Service is *(Spells)* R-o-a-c-h. It's pronounced "Ro-ach."

ROOSTER. Roach, no way!

IRENE. *(Correcting him)* "Ro-ach" wants to buy up Daddy's marshes.

ROOSTER. Do we have to talk about money and ruin cocktails?

IRENE. Listen, you might learn something. It's hardly possible.

ROOSTER. *(Gnaws a piece of celery)* I feel like I'm swimming upstream.

IRENE. "Ro-ach" needs a thirty-year net lease on my rear property. *(Pause)* This will affect your grandchildren. My attorney has reservations. The land would be worth much more if sold commercially.

ROOSTER. We've heard all this before.

IRENE. I'm trying to get to what happened last week.

ROOSTER. By returning to the beginning? Every person has a lifelong conversation with himself. What am I but an alien point of view entering your conversation?

IRENE. Right! I do better with folks who can't talk back, babies, people in a coma. That's why I volunteer at the hospital. Once the coma victims start getting better, they're difficult to deal with. Irresponsible!

*(**IRENE** takes a Bloody Mary. **QUINT** enters. He cradles the phone and searches for the paper.)*

QUINT. No, I haven't seen the business section.

IRENE. That's why I've put the whole preserve idea on hold.

QUINT. *(Shocked, to **IRENE**)* You said you were reconsidering.

IRENE. I don't remember anything of the sort! *(Deferentially)* Won't you join us for cocktails, Quint?

QUINT. *(Hanging up the phone)* No, thanks. I've got to see what the Times has to say about the real estate market. Doesn't anybody bring in the paper?

SOLITAIRE

IRENE. They keep throwing it in the duck pond. We should cancel the subscription. *(Sipping the drink)* There is too much Tabasco in this Bloody Mary, Roo. Taste it?

*(**SOUND**: There is a moaning sound, like a baby crying, as **BUNKY** returns from the yard.)*

BUNKY. A tomcat. He followed me from the woods. I named him Phantom.

IRENE. Ye gods! He's stuck in the walls.

BUNKY. He's been there for three days.

IRENE. Quint, you should keep Bunky out of those woods.

QUINT. Phantom. *(Exits for the paper, mumbling)* That's some name. Phantom.

*(**SOUND**: The cat groans faintly from inside the walls.)*

IRENE. *(Takes another Bloody Mary and draws deeply through the straw)* Bunky, there's too much hot sauce in the Bloody Marys.

BUNKY. Is there anything I can do to earn money here? Straighten the garage?

IRENE. I'll pay you to leave my house alone. Y'all put your glasses back.

BUNKY. *(Collects the glasses)* I feel like a bean bag thrown back and forth.

IRENE. *(Rises)* You're my only hope. Your father's one step ahead of the sheriff, and Rooster's totally lazy.

*(**IRENE** and **BUNKY** exit for the kitchen. **QUINT**'s phone rings.)*

ROOSTER. Another arrow. Being respectful doesn't mean you invite a massacre.

*(**ROOSTER** picks up the pearls, pockets them, and retreats to the beach.)*

QUINT. *(Returning)* I'm so disgusted, Roo. I'm not reading a wet newspaper. I have certain standards of cleanliness...*(Changes his voice to answer the phone)* No, Quint is not here. You'll have to collect payment. *(Talking naturally)* Oh, Jay, it's me, Quint. They're drilling offshore? Sift through the oil companies...see who wants a track of marshland. A guy named Fatswell's been sniffing around.

(SOUND: An alarm blasts.)

(QUINT hangs up the phone. BUNKY rushes in.)

QUINT. Boon's triggered the alarm. How do you stop the dang thing? Is there a switch! *(BUNKY laughs)* I'm not laughing! You think it's funny, but these sirens are giving me high blood pressure!

BUNKY. Push the red button, the panic button, then 34960. The code's *(Spells)* F-O-O-L.

(SOUND: Irene's phone rings. Quint answers it.)

QUINT. Fool! Not you, stupid. It's...the code word, FOOL.

BUNKY. Not fool. *(Spells as he exits laughing)* F-O-O-L.

QUINT. *(Spells)* F-O-O-L.

(SOUND: The alarm stops. We hear someone strolling up the drive, whistling through her teeth.)

(QUINT leans out the gallery.)

QUINT. Jasmine! Welcome to Serenity. *(Hangs up the phone)* You're a one-woman parade.

(JASMINE enters, dangling her custom-made shoes over her shoulder and dragging glamorous luggage.)

JASMINE. My driver dropped me at the gate. This house is a fortress. It looks like a fat lady who's been to the orthodontist. All that metal work!

QUINT. We're broke, but safe!

JASMINE. I want a ride in your big, bad Jaguar.

QUINT. Sold it.

JASMINE. I can't think of you without a Jaguar. It's part of who you are. *(She peers out)* I can't find it. It used to be I could find your car right away. *(Pointing)*

It's not that old raggedy thing by the duck pond. You're driving a Japanese subcompact!

QUINT. A rental car, darling. I should have sold my interests in the company. Then I could drive a BMW instead of a Saab—which is in the repair shop.

JASMINE. *(Removing her gloves)* I'm a parts model. I might break a nail! I flew home via New York. Elizabeth Arden. They sent me through the revolving door and voilà!

QUINT. Voilà!

JASMINE. I believe one should always dress as rich as possible. I want my clothes to make a fashion statement, and these clothes definitely talk! *(She spins around)*

QUINT. *(Seductively, pants like a dog)* Arf! Arf!

JASMINE. They're from a shoot in Australia! I don't like to encourage foreigners, but I do like variety in my clothes.

QUINT. You remind me of my ex before therapy made her so difficult.

JASMINE. I like dressing up and dressing down. I don't like dressing in the middle.

QUINT. You don't?

JASMINE. I've joined Debtors Anonymous. This group of shopping addicts. But, I can't stop myself. When I see something I want, I buy it. I've run up an incredible bill on Pete's company Visa.

QUINT. Pete?

JASMINE. Daddy Dubonnet...

QUINT. You said "Pete."

BUNKY. *(Enters and plops down another tray of Bloody Marys)* Running back and forth between yesterday and today. Hey, Jasmine! I saw your hands on "General Hospital" and "One Life to Live." *(Reaches for* **JASMINE***'s hands)*

JASMINE. *(Slips her hands in her pockets)* These fingers are insured against chapping. When I'm broke, they go to work.

BUNKY. I taped your "Silk n' Soft. I'm Dripping Charisma!" commercials.

JASMINE. I'm sorry I missed the funeral. We were in the middle of shooting. No one would accept my collect calls...Did Mimi like my red blanket—for the casket?

BUNKY. No! She said you charged it to her.

JASMINE. I'm paying her back. Thanks for the rose you had laminated in plastic. Smells sweet. Such a pretty purple.

BUNKY. Now, Mimi...always talks "property."

QUINT. Relatives are not like property. Property is valued in this family.

*(SOUND: A squeal comes from **JASMINE**'s luggage.)*

JASMINE. It's my Yorkshire Terrier.

QUINT. Not another pet!

JASMINE. Cornelia Bronte Shambles. The smallest dog alive. She's ninety-seven, and can't control her bladder. She just lifts her skirts and goes anywhere. *(Shaking her little bag)* See!

QUINT. Put her up, son.

BUNKY. Inside?

JASMINE. Leave her in the top drawer in my back room. She won't wet there. My underwear is more sacred to her than all your Orientals.

*(**BUNKY** exits with the dog. **JASMINE** meanders about.)*

QUINT. Have a Bloody Mary.

JASMINE. Just water for me. Caviar on toast. Marvelous. *(Savors the caviar, then tosses it into the trash)*

IRENE. *(Entering, she stalks* **JASMINE**) I wondered how long it'd take you to show up.

JASMINE. Mama Dubonnet! *(***JASMINE** *puts her hands in her pockets)* Just picking! I…I…I have "fear of fat." All my friends are fat, bald, married with kids. I don't eat; I graze. I can get as much satisfaction from looking. Really!

IRENE. You're on a diet?

JASMINE. It's not a diet. It's a way of life. When I get hungry, I eat a banana. Quint, could you peel this?

IRENE. Jasmine, you still live on the same postage stamp? You've got to drive thirty-five miles into the brushes, Quint, to get to her house.

ROOSTER. *(Stumbles in, in a hiking outfit, shirt unbuttoned)* Wow! What started as a walk ended up an adventure! Oh, hi, Jasmine.

*(***BUNKY** *dashes onstage with a pot of steaming fish soup.)*

BUNKY. Gumbo is served! Jazz, will you recite something from a movie later?

JASMINE. No. *(Twitches* **BUNKY***'s ear and whispers)* They don't pay the entertainment in this family, like they don't pay the help.

IRENE. We certainly do pay the help, even when they don't show up!

(Everyone sits. **IRENE** *signals for* **BUNKY** *to say "Grace." He does so, rapidly, with no emotion, then they dive into dinner.)*

QUINT. My boy got 1570 on his SAT, a near perfect score, but something's missing. Sewannee, the University of the South, said: "Nothing in his application sparked their interest."

ROOSTER. It's chronic fatigue syndrome. A yuppie disease from having too many college applications. He's allergic to the twenty-first century.

BUNKY. Ha! That's good.

QUINT. I should have sent Bunky to that military school in Alabama…where the colonel comes to your house to get you!

BUNKY. I was voted the boy most likely to die from a violent death.
(Phone rings.)

IRENE. *(Pauses, taunting* **QUINT***)* It's for you, Quint.

QUINT. *(Withdrawing with the phone)* Where? Who?...DeBango wants a Dunn and Brad report from the New York Stock Exchange on me?

ROOSTER. Have you got any Pick-a-pepper sauce?

IRENE. Roo's problem in life is he jokes too much, and of course you have to eat.

ROOSTER. Pick-a-pepper! Yum!

IRENE. He puts that sauce on everything.

ROOSTER. Some sauces have flavor, but pepper is what makes a sauce great.

IRENE. You have to hit him in the head with a two-by-four like a jackass to get him to stop. Either way he'll have to answer to God, not just to his mother.

ROOSTER. "Gran Sangre de Tore." Great blood of the bull! Yum! Conversation isn't just talk, it's blood sport if it's worth having!

IRENE. Be careful, Roo. I could cut you completely out of the will.

ROOSTER. You insult me and forbid me to react.

IRENE. I don't compete with preadolescent mouths. Bad taste doesn't condone politeness. *(Puts down her fork and wipes her eyes)* I don't know why I go to all this trouble to create Sunday dinner.

BUNKY. For me, Mimi. Excellent turkey gumbo.

ROOSTER. *(Eats and talks simultaneously)* I fill up here, so I can starve on my own money.

IRENE. Don't eat with your fingers, Roo.

ROOSTER. I've got plenty of ice in my refrigerator, but no food.

SOLITAIRE

IRENE. Close your mouth, son.

ROOSTER. Whenever I rent a movie at the video store, they say, "You're late on your payments."

IRENE. You can't socialize with the manners of a pig.

ROOSTER. *(Gulps his wine out of the bottle)* That cheap box won't hold two bottles of wine! Ha.

IRENE. You come to the table with your gut hanging out.

ROOSTER. *(Adjusting his cap)* When I go out, I look presentable.

IRENE. There is a code of behavior in acceptable society. You eat with your fingers. Talk with your mouth open. Drink nonstop!

ROOSTER. I've got to fill up with booze to sit at this table. Like a blowfish, I inflate until I burst. There are dead blowfish shattered all over the beach. Being polluted to death. They swell up because they're terrified...expand until they pop. But it's not worth it for one meal ticket! *(Dumps his plate over)* For one lousy meal, it's not!

IRENE. I'm so mad at Pete. He went and died on me. He used to handle this. I'm the easiest person in the world to get along with. You can ask my dead husband. *(Exiting)* Clean up, Bunky.

BUNKY. My night hasn't begun until I've picked up somebody's shit. Good night.

(SOUND: Music. A dreary version of "Columbia, the Gem of the Ocean" drifts in from Star of the Sea.)

QUINT. *(Sips coffee and peers into his cup)* No, it's not a good night. It's another lousy night.

(BUNKY mops up the drenched table. JASMINE flips her address book.)

JASMINE. *(Seizing a phone as if it's a life preserver)* Being around this family in the country...It's the saturation that gets to you.

QUINT. Coffee?

JASMINE. That stuff is toxic!

(JASMINE hands **QUINT** *a phone, and he punches in the number.* **JASMINE***'s hand slides over* **QUINT***'s when taking the receiver.)*

JASMINE. Is this the Hilton? The Hilton that has the rain forest? Don't put me on hold! Shit!...Get me Chuck Feingold, Big Star Productions. No, I won't wait! This is long distance! *(Presses the phone against her shoulder)* This receptionist from hell!

*(**SOUND**: The phone rings,* **JASMINE** *grabs it.)*

JASMINE. Oh, Chuckie...What?...Who put 'Midnight Rapture' on hold? It's canceled...Oh, no. How can I advance you the money? Good night, "poochie poops." *(**JASMINE** slams down the phone, and forgetting her hands, rips open her purse.)*

QUINT. Try some coffee.

JASMINE. I've already drunk my allotted cup.

QUINT. Ah, ha! Middle age has you in its claw—you're counting coffee cups.

JASMINE. *(She massages her nails ferociously)* I need a loufa sponge and a herbal wrap to lift the dead cells! I can't believe this fat vein. Yeek, a ripped nail!

QUINT. After thirty, y'all have to hang up your spurs.

JASMINE. I've peaked. I know I'm old. My hands are old. I'm two years older than God.

QUINT. Nature discriminates!

JASMINE. Men discriminate! The biggest part of acting is attitude. And Doctor Wiseman can't find the right pills.

QUINT. There's a bankruptcy every five minutes. For sale signs like postage stamps stuck on houses along the beach. I can't relate to your cosmetic problems.

JASMINE. Those deals don't concern me.

QUINT. Well, they must pay you a lot for M.C.ing the L.A., S.P.C.A. dog walkathon?

JASMINE. It's volunteer work.

BUNKY. That's not a salaried position.

JASMINE. Mama Dubonnet told me I didn't have to trouble myself with any family meetings. It's a simple will.

QUINT. On paper, yes, but in practice...This is the last outpost where people make a will prioritizing the adults they can control. Without this agenda, everyone scatters. It's time you get your own attorney instead of relying on this family's.

JASMINE. What can I do at six on a Sunday?

BUNKY. *(Swatting the air)* Nasty horseflies.

*(***JASMINE** *inches over so her breasts almost touch the middle button of* **QUINT***'s starched shirt.)*

JASMINE. Can we talk tacky? Daddy Dubonnet promised me ten million dollars for this picture.

BUNKY. Mimi won't like "Midnight Rapture"!

JASMINE. When I decide to do something, I pick up and do it. You don't have to show me more than once!

BUNKY. Another horsefly.

QUINT. We must make haste—slowly for two reasons. There's no forced heirship in Louisiana, and you are an adopted child.

JASMINE. She won't cut me out!

QUINT. You're tough! Good.

(A horsefly spins overhead, but **QUINT** *catches it in his fist and squashes it midair.)*

QUINT. You'll need that resistance because here everything's changed. The only thing a bear respects is a bigger bear.

(SOUND: A phone blares. JASMINE goes to get it, but QUINT puts his hand over the receiver.)

QUINT. Keep 'em dangling. That'll keep 'em interested. *(Tracing a question mark on her hand)* Warm hands.

JASMINE. Cold heart.

BUNKY. *(Throwing napkins on to a tray)* Mimi says, "If it looks like a duck, walks like a duck, and quacks like a duck, it's probably a duck."

(QUINT marches back to the table, pulls out an alligator-skin checkbook, and scribbles a check.)

QUINT. Get yourselves some fireworks. *(Tosses him some keys)* Drive below eighty.

BUNKY. Quackidy quack! *(Skips out)*

JASMINE. Mama Dubonnet's scared of me because I've got insanity in my blood. There's nothing I'm afraid of. My real daddy was a crazy man. Pushed me in the Mississippi River when I sassed him. So I've seen the rush of death. When Pete adopted me, I weighed eighty-nine pounds. My stomach was so swollen it looked like a balloon. But Pete loved lost causes. We went walking every Sunday. Pete treated me like a treasure.

QUINT. *(Removing his jacket and tie)* You weren't one of the secretaries he slung against the couch...who made "her" walk blindfolded.

JASMINE. He preferred me to his real son and daughter.

QUINT. Relationships for him were like ducks in a shooting gallery. He knocked one down and another popped up in its place. No wonder Roo's so screwed up.

JASMINE. You're responsible for Roo. He's imitating you. Following some penchant for power, disguised by psychological bullshit!

QUINT. I don't have to take this from a hand model!

JASMINE. I'm more than a hand model. I had a T.V. series! I did commercials—temporarily. Now they've become my specialty. But for how long? Even silicone injections won't stop veins from popping up. There are no hand lifts. I want to work. To do that, I need massive plastic surgery, a liposuction, and ten million dollars. Well, just think about it. I deserve the money!

*(**SOUND**: Low romantic music floats under the scene.)*

JASMINE. I know you weren't there for...Kitten.

QUINT. My wife? She left me. Sailed to France with her new independence! Maybe husband number two will thaw her out.

JASMINE. You cheated on her.

QUINT. Once Kitten returned to college, she never came to bed. Students arrived at the house in groups like tourists.

JASMINE. You were outnumbered.

QUINT. I would sit up at night watching your movies. "Boys Night Out," "Color Me Red," "Slippery Sunday," and remembering those slow summers. I should have left my wife then, but Bunky fell ill. Wasted away to a little pile of bones on a chair. You make concessions.

JASMINE. Too many concessions.

QUINT. Sex is a tyrant. It pops up its head and demands your flesh. *(He touches her back.)*

JASMINE. Stay away, Satan! Just because somebody liked it once doesn't mean they'll like it again.

QUINT. I'm new and improved. *(**QUINT** twitches her ear.)*

JASMINE. This is wrong!

QUINT. Does it feel wrong?

JASMINE. Not now, but maybe later.

*(**JASMINE** and **QUINT** kiss. **IRENE** observes from a side door.)*

QUINT. *(Putting his arm around JASMINE)* Let's go to the beach.

JASMINE. Okay, but don't touch me. Just don't touch me. *(They both exit.)*

(BUNKY enters loaded with fireworks, followed by IRENE.)

BUNKY. I've got cherry bombs, snakes, hand grenades! *(Dumps them and calls)* Hey, Roo! It's going to be a battlefield! Roo! Better tie Boon up! He'll get his face blown off if he sniffs around these fireworks.

IRENE. I can't take one more forced celebration.

BUNKY. Where's Roo?

IRENE. He'll be better in the morning. I should be panicked, but it's all in a day's work.

BUNKY. Did he have another spell?

IRENE. Since Roo was born, I have ceased to be Mrs. Dubonnet. I am Rooster's mother. *(Wipes her mascara)* I live with an inner panic button stuck on alert.

(IRENE picks up the sketchbook. She has the urge to rip it up, but she rests it on the table.)

IRENE. He's becoming too…sensitive. I realize some parts of society don't consider white males useful, but this family needs one. I might as well do a fire dance. I tried to be sweet to him. I don't need him.

BUNKY. He's painting his signature work!

IRENE. Art's consuming him.

BUNKY. *(Reverently opening the sketch book)* Such talent!

IRENE. Depraved drawings. Talent is something the world decides about us later. It's not anything we can know in our heart. Artists have lives, they don't have careers.

(LIGHTS: Bonfires blaze from the beach.)

SOLITAIRE

(BUNKY picks up the binoculars and crosses downstage.)

BUNKY. They're starting up some bonfires! Wow, will you look at that!

IRENE. Try looking for a happy artist.

BUNKY. Don't start, Mimi.

IRENE. I just try to keep on going with some quality. That's not easy. I've been a mother longer than you realize. Motherhood is a series of letdowns. The same old conversations, rushing to nowhere. When I'm really mad at my son, I ignore his drawings. He gets back at me by drawing, incessantly. Art allows him to punish me in a disguised fashion. The amount of carnage created by him is immeasurable. I don't think mothers ever truly forgive what sons do to them.

BUNKY. Don't get paranoid.

IRENE. Roo's growing suited to the life of an artist. He's developing the mettle for cruelty.

BUNKY. Sure is hot! I like the smell of summer. These scorching July nights.

IRENE. I have spent forty years of my life building my name in this community. I don't want it destroyed by this garbage.

BUNKY. I don't care how hot it gets.

IRENE. Stray artists rattling around in the French Quarter like dice in a cup. You have to breathe life in them. They're so drugged. Most decent people don't go into the Quarter anymore.

BUNKY. But sometimes with three lines he'll make me homesick for a place.

IRENE. If I want a painting, I want a real painting. I don't want an overgrown cat or some fish guts.

BUNKY. He's trying to tell a story. Try to understand. *(Exits)*

IRENE. Vile images. That's art. *(Swoops up the sketchbook)* It's the freak show characters that push this trash. Damaged personalities. Obsessed with the obscene. There's nothing lonelier than being the mother of an artist. I got a lot more by being mean than by being kind.

(IRENE begins tearing up the pages.)

*(**SOUND**: Phantom moans in the walls.)*

IRENE. Still alive, are you? *(Exits to the beach.)*

Scene Three

(The next day, July Fourth, twilight. **QUINT** *is wearing a T-shirt, "He who has the most toys wins," and fixing a crab trap. Sporting a bird-watching outfit,* **JASMINE** *is manipulating a telescope overlooking the Gulf.* **BUNKY** *is stretched out, filling out job applications. Nearby a silver tray of scotch and bourbon, a bucket of ice, and leftover donuts, croissants, and coffee idle on a table. The sun is setting—red fire bleeding through the sky. The Star of the Sea Angelus resounds as* **ROOSTER** *limps into the room. He looks half dead.)*

ROOSTER. *(Reaches for a donut and searches around the room)* A three-donut day! Got to jump-start that body. My eating habits are terrible, and I'm not going to change them...

JASMINE. That's stupid.

ROOSTER. Sometimes it's better to be stupid. Smart people realize we can't figure things out. *(Collapses—throwing his leg across the arm of a chair)* I keep forgetting where I put things!

QUINT. *(Shocked by* **ROO***'s leg)* You've got a lump that big on your ankle!

ROOSTER. Whenever you're sick, you must face the wheel of fortune.

BUNKY. He could need a transfusion, Dad!

ROOSTER. I don't want blood.

JASMINE. Please!

QUINT. *(Noticing streaks on* **ROO***'s ankle)* God, you're turning pink in spots. Bleeding through the skin. Hold out your foot. Oh, my God...

ROOSTER. Spider bites. We are all terminal! As soon as it's out, people start treating you differently. I have something wrong with my chart, but they can't tell what it is. I can't find my paintings!

QUINT. You should stay off that foot.

ROOSTER. Find my sketchbook, Quint. I haven't drawn anything today...I need that book to see where I left off with my life. It's got all the memories that I've been collecting, like the sensations in the leaves when the sky turns white in July.

JASMINE. Just draw them again.

ROOSTER. You think my memory can sustain these details?

QUINT. Maybe they're not so important.

ROOSTER. *(His throat is rasping)* You act like my sketchbook's a calendar or something. It's not a fucking date book, y'all! See the dentist. Repair the car. Have lunch with Mama.

*(Nudging **BUNKY** to patronize **ROO**, **QUINT** pretends to be bidding at an auction.)*

QUINT. I'll offer a ten-dollar reward!

BUNKY. I'll add five to that!

ROOSTER. Y'all think I can start, stop like some computer. I know painting doesn't ring up the checking account.

QUINT. Make it fifteen, fifteen, fifteen, no, twenty dollars.

ROOSTER. No one's going to furnish my office or buy me a desk.

JASMINE. Here's twenty-five.

ROOSTER. Twenty-five dollars for the entire series! It's amazing I'm still in my right mind!

*(**SOUND**: A group of the town's boys are parading along the beach, playing something like, "When the Saints Go Marching In.")*

*(**QUINT** and **JASMINE** begin dancing, waving hankies, doing the cake walk. The strained sounds of their dancing shoot through **ROO**'s heart, calling him to task for his lost youth.)*

ROOSTER. That band again! I've got to reconstruct my life...the past week.

BUNKY. *(Steering **ROO** offstage)* Let's check out front.

QUINT. Poor bastard.

JASMINE. *(Dancing with* **QUINT***)* Don't let Roo's theatrics worry you. You should feel sorry for me, stranded in the boondocks...You could sprout roots here from just lying around. If I don't keep busy, I rot like the trees. My idea of fun is lounging by a pool in the Beverly Hills Hotel. I don't ask for much: elegance, someone nice to talk to, like Julia Roberts. God, I miss *(cont.)* Los Angeles! Let's go to the beach! Watch the birds visiting for the day. Sandpipers are going extinct! They're mating on the beach.

QUINT. In exile.

JASMINE. It's part tradition, part assumption, part desperation. Come on. Let the sunset caress our skin. The water's pearly— blues, grays, all shades of gray. See the waves...lapping everywhere...and foam!

QUINT. A done deal! Watch out for that ant hill covered with poison.

JASMINE. Look at the clover all over and honeysuckle. *(Offstage, their ripples of laughter trail off)*

ROOSTER. *(Wanders onstage with a wildflower)* I discovered this red honeysuckle. It has no scent. I'll study one fragile, delicate vine. Memories are all I have left.

*(****SOUND****: The phone rings off the hook.)*

BUNKY. We'll find those sketches. Don't worry.

IRENE. *(Shrieking offstage)* Bunky, run get the phone!

BUNKY. I've never run for anything in my life. *(Answers the phone like a calloused receptionist)* She's not here. It's for Quint. He's not here. *(Slams down the phone)* I'm right on the edge.

*(****IRENE*** *hurries onstage to the howling of dogs. She looks unusually glamorous and uneasy with her Panama hat in one hand and a paper bag in the other.)*

IRENE. This place sounds more and more like an animal shelter. *(She pops off her jewelry and shrieks)* Quint! Jasmine!

*(****ROOSTER*** *has set himself up with a fantastic oil lamp and a fifth of Jack Daniels.)*

(LIGHTS: Moonlight streams across his face. Periodically, firecrackers, Roman candles, and smoke bombs sizzle in the sky. **ROOSTER** *rings a bell.)*

IRENE. Ruthie May.

ROOSTER. The seven o'clock cry. Every twenty-four hours, she screams from the heart.

IRENE. *(Hunting around)* I've mislaid my pearls, son. Can you help me find them? I guess I'll have to crawl on my hands and knees. Well, say something!

ROOSTER. What day is it?

IRENE. Monday!

ROOSTER. All day?

IRENE. Don't you like that?

ROOSTER. *(Swigs his drink)* I have to be loaded Monday, or I won't come home.

IRENE. You're at it again.

ROOSTER. This isn't me. I'm standing in for a friend. Do you know who I am? Well, neither do I. Do you know where my money is? Well, you don't know much.

IRENE. *(Rooting around for the pearls)* I've had experience with weepy eccentric people. Spoilt, we used to call them. Don't let the normalcy of my life interrupt your creativity.

(SOUND: There is a deadly silence.)

(LIGHTS: Moonbeams begin falling like diamonds across the gallery. Around it, Spanish daggers, palmettos, banana trees are starting to stretch their jagged limbs toward the moonlight. Roman candles explode streamers of red, lavender, and silver through the sky.)

IRENE. Actually, I came out here to accept your apology. A poor peace is better than an excellent war. Such a starry night. It's a blue moon, the second full moon in a month. They said forty percent chance of rain tonight, and it's beautiful! Remember that game we played on the pier, "Light My Candle"? One person runs from corner to corner saying, "Light my candle," and everybody switches seats behind him screaming, "Next door, neighbor!"

(LIGHTS: Roman candles shoot over the Gulf, exploding color everywhere.)

(SOUND: Fireworks crackle like pork skins frying; sizzling, hissing.)

IRENE. Come watch the Roman candles?

ROOSTER. I hear them.

IRENE. It's easy to start drinking, son, but when do you stop? The wee hours of the morning.

ROOSTER. It's better to drink with steam coming out your ears.

IRENE. I read about a commercial artist who makes three million a video. He's outlined five steps to success: be brief, be winning...

ROOSTER. If there are so few steps, why isn't everyone successful? *(Drinks violently)* Some artists are happier if they don't see their paintings hung.

IRENE. It's time to switch when you begin losing your hair! No one's ever going to hang your painting!

ROOSTER. Watercolors.

IRENE. Painting, watercolor, whatever.

(ROOSTER taps his foot, a habit that reminds her of his nervous breakdown.)

(LIGHTS: Moonlight streams across his face.)

ROOSTER. Never stare down a fish because they have no eyelids.

IRENE. No eyelids!

ROOSTER. You're a loudspeaker. I whisper something in your ear and it comes out your mouth.

IRENE. I dislike seeing you sick.

ROOSTER. It could be worse. I could be dead. My nervous breakdown hasn't healed.

IRENE. Shh. Depression.

ROOSTER. I need a few days off from the world to recover each week.

IRENE. You want to rent that villa in Italy? Take a Mediterranean Cruise. What do you want?

ROOSTER. When did this shrinkage of your mind occur? You started smart. Valedictorian. But you've been thinking the same thoughts for thirty years. I have no more status than a parlor entertainer.

IRENE. I'd hoped you had enough distractions with the textbook.

ROOSTER. Distractions! Is that what you call my work?

IRENE. You have to face reality, son.

ROOSTER. Do you think people walked on the moon by doing that? I'm like Cassandra, balancing the gift of prophecy with the curse of madness. Despite blistering summers, I'm drawing every species of vegetation, animal, and insect. I have penetrated the thickets on hands and knees. Slept in lagoons to make my perception of nature's paradise.

IRENE. Pipe dreams! You're living in a pipe? Who's bought one drawing but me?

ROOSTER. You have a bad mouth and you say cruel things to people.

IRENE. You've got to paint in a style closer to the center where the majority is.

ROOSTER. I'd rather go back to the hospital.

IRENE. The curator of the museum said plain as day, your style has…no appeal.

ROOSTER. He promised to hang one piece.

IRENE. If I give him five hundred thousand dollars. It's your connections he's after. You said, "Teaching interests me."

ROOSTER. *(Tapping his foot)* I don't want to as-ss-ociate with those people!

IRENE. Why not catalog slides at the Historic Collection?

ROOSTER. Still trying to buy me that job!

IRENE. You could work at your dad's agency.

ROOSTER. *(Chugs more Jack Daniels)* I've received an ancient legacy. A commission! I can't think of myself as not being an artist. Painting either brings you to the cocktail circuit or to God.

IRENE. You don't dress like a priest.

ROOSTER. I practice to get it right. One aspect of perfection.

IRENE. And what aspect is that?

ROOSTER. Dodging the predators. That isn't easy because the laws of the sea don't apply. Out there, the predators have names: the electric eel, the swordfish, the hammerhead shark. Here, humans are perverse. They poison the artist through emotional blackmail. You've got loved ones like piranha hungering to extract your talent. Going into a frenzy for a drop of genius. A piranha's teeth snap like a steel jaw. You don't stop one by patting its head, Mother. I survive by keeping a low profile like a flatfish, pressed to the sea floor. I was born like a regular human, but my eyes have rolled around to the top of my head from crawling along the bottom. It's easier for me to change me than for me to change you.

(ROOSTER stretches out on the floor with the whiskey bottle.)

(LIGHTS: Automatic yard lights flash on silently as if some god has magically lit up the gallery like an exhibition hall.)

(SOUND: The radio inside plays something like Henry Purcell's "La Mort du Roi"—its haunting sounds blend with the rising wind.)

IRENE. You and I were close before.

ROOSTER. Before, I was inclined to do what you wanted me to do.

IRENE. I don't see life as a series of victimizations.

*(***ROOSTER** *starts to draw—valuing the light replacing the dusk.)*

IRENE. You've drawn for a while. Why not move on to something else?

ROOSTER. Did you find my sketches?

IRENE. I prayed about them at Star of the Sea. Father Fannen talked about families living in cardboard boxes. One person losing some sketches is not terminal.

ROOSTER. It's not terminal, but I can see it from here.

IRENE. You're punishing yourself over something no one appreciates…it's like wanting to play a symphony in a barroom south of Houma in a place called "Whiskey Pass." Ha! Ha!

ROOSTER. People are things, Mama. Artists! Ax murderers! You don't like my sketches because they reveal too much about the endowed violence of this family…

IRENE. I found your sketches. I didn't want to give them to you until I had them fixed.

*(***ROOSTER** *peers in the bag as if it contains a rotting corpse. He extracts bits of wet paper—wiping his hands on his pants and shaking his head.* **ROOSTER** *limps around the table looking at this piece and at that in an attempt to salvage something.)*

ROOSTER. Oh God no! They're torn to pieces. Drenched! Where did you find them?

IRENE. On the beach.

ROOSTER. When?

IRENE. A few hours ago.

ROOSTER. I can't repair these sketches. I never realized there was a time clock for artists. In the wee morning eye of night, I feel like I'm in this river of fire. Millions of artists are screaming, "Help!"

IRENE. Please! I'm not a vicious person.

(SOUND: We hear the lapping of the waves in the distance and the buzzing of locusts circling the house.)

(ROOSTER watches her, sensing her uneasiness like a dog spotting a cat.)

ROOSTER. You tore them up, didn't you? You think what's yours is yours, and what's mine is yours. You were afraid my artwork might bring me glory. Independence that would distance me from you.

IRENE. *(Flattening the wrinkles in her designer skirt)* You want to blame someone...all right, blame me.

ROOSTER. Cut my heart out! It's all right, Ma.

IRENE. Son, I'm trying to protect you. Do you want to go back to the hospital?

ROOSTER. *(The pain in his leg firing him to attack her)* Vulture! You go through the motions of motherhood, the meals, the stories, the meetings. You never missed one. But underneath the fuss, you're a buzzard, mangling the weak without a pause of remorse. You feed on the dying. Suck up feelings. Hook yourself into another's flesh and rip. We are responsible for each other's soul. You have annihilated my self-esteem.

(IRENE crosses, weak-kneed, and with all the power in her manicured hand slaps him.)

IRENE. I'm your mother.

(ROOSTER grabs his face and sinks back, catching himself on the table and crashing over the scotch and bourbon, donuts, and bucket of ice. **ROOSTER** *sinks down into a chair, depression weighing like a coat of steel over him. Seizes sketches from under the alcohol and olives. Dumps the scraps back in the soiled bag.)*

ROOSTER. I wish you'd never given me life! I don't believe life is real. It's a big movie written, produced, and directed by God. If I thought my life was real, I'd blow my brains out! *(Shoves the bag at his mother)* Put it out back with the plastic bags and the bottle tops. Pollution!

IRENE. Get drunk, indulge yourself. Life is a big soap opera and you're the star!

ROOSTER. *(Removes the pearls from his pocket)* Here, strangle your neck like you strangle everybody else's!

IRENE. You're drunk!

ROOSTER. I'm drunk, and you're a bitch, but I'll be sober in the morning.

*(**LIGHTS:** Sparkles flash in the sky.)*

*(**ROOSTER** begins ripping her pearls and spraying them across the gallery.)*

(curtain act one)

SOLITAIRE

ACT TWO

Scene One

(Four o'clock on a Sunday afternoon, a week later. The furniture is draped in white duck cloth, and the chandelier wrapped in netting. A day-bed canopied with gauze protects the patient, **ROOSTER***, from mosquitoes. Near it is a mammoth bowl of goldfish that* **BUNKY** *feeds periodically. Dead leaves from a recent squall are scattered around some plants. The stereo resounds something like Henry Purcell's "La Mort du Roi." Its lament blends with the rising wind and waves. Moments later,* **BUNKY** *bounds down the stairs, acting out a blues song to amuse* **ROOSTER***.)*

IRENE. Bunky, turn off that music!

*(***SOUND***:* **BUNKY** *flicks off the blues and hides. Seeing the gaunt expression on* **ROO***'s face,* **IRENE** *cringes.)*

IRENE. Roo. I've never understood motherhood. Bruised camellias are all I've successfully nursed. We found someone to repair your paintings—a disaster specialist from Orlando, Florida.

*(***IRENE** *folds back some cheesecloth.* **ROO** *coughs again, responding to an eerie sound, like trembling shutters.)*

IRENE. Who's there? *(Spots* **BUNKY***)* Bunky, stop eavesdropping.

BUNKY. *(Staring over at* **ROO***)* I can't rest. I closed my eyes and I felt violated. Uncle Roo looks so...weak.

BUNKY. Every time he veges out, I'm afraid he'll never come back...

IRENE. Most patients improve at home where they recognize their surroundings...These Mississippi doctors have just learned that. They're from nothing. Climbing with both hands. My great-great-grandfather was a surgeon in the Civil War, and he knew that.

*(***IRENE** *ensconces herself at a tiny table. She begins shuffling cards.)*

IRENE. Don't you want to play cards?

BUNKY. Card games are boring.

IRENE. Their predictability is comforting. Solitaire's a game one person can play. Thank God, since that's the direction the world's going in.

BUNKY. Did Doctor Boudreau call?

IRENE. No. Solitaire's the American name; the English term is Patience.

BUNKY. Face up, Mimi. With his allergies, it could be the beginning of the end.

IRENE. A King of Spades—the black suit again. There are so many medical decisions to make in a lifetime. You can afford to get a few wrong; you still come out ahead.

BUNKY. Father Fannen wants to give him Extreme Unction, Mimi!

IRENE. The Sacrament of the Sick, not the dead! All sickness does not go on to death, son.

(ROOSTER moans. BUNKY runs his fingers through his hair.)

BUNKY. Listen!...Is he having trouble breathing? He's so swollen.

IRENE. The doctors are taking him to Oschner Clinic tomorrow for more tests.

BUNKY. You never told me! That clinic is terrible. Needles and tubes everywhere!

IRENE. *(Aligning a sequence of spade cards)* Your sophomoric ideas on medicine don't interest me.

BUNKY. Shit. He'll just get worse there. No one empties the garbage, they yell in the hallways, and patients keep buzzing for nurses. It's like being in a cage at a zoo. People pass you with curiosity. But when you need someone, you can't get help.

IRENE. *(Mechanically plays a new hand of Solitaire)* That's not true.

BUNKY. Not when you're there, of course. You barely touch the buzzer and they fly in like hawks. It's your money they're after. Unfortunately, the sick are less attractive. They moan from meal to meal like broken screws in some machine. And their food is like crap. I used all my allowance sneaking Grandpa fast food—

in case you'd care to know. Fine, Mimi. You want to make a pincushion out of Roo, then don't come bawling to me. I won't start dialing specialists from New York and L.A. like we did for Grandpa...after it's too late. I'm not going to get hysterical or anything. I'm just moving out.

IRENE. I'm the responsible party. Not you.

BUNKY. I'm the only member of this family willing to face reality. Uncle Roo's a hypochondriac. I heard one doctor say it. Roo gets sick to get attention, because when he's healthy, people won't let up on him.

IRENE. Grandpa was right—he was always warning me about letting you get too bossy.

BUNKY. Rooster wants to stay home on the couch. Jasmine and I can rotate taking care of him.

IRENE. Jasmine! Ha! She spends her time mixing her mud mask and dousing her fingers in oil.

BUNKY. *(Paces nervously about)* When I nurse him, he gets better. Today he asked me if I fed Boon.

JASMINE. *(Rushing in)* Damn! Greta almost bit me.

IRENE. Even well-fed pets will hunt for the fun of it.

JASMINE. *(Screams, bending over her and shaking her hair like a mop)* Something's loose, an extension.

IRENE. Jasmine, stop emoting. Read something to Roo from *Remembrance of Things Past*.

JASMINE. Not now! My hair's falling out! Does it have to break off?

IRENE. You lack stamina! You haven't faced the vilest quarters of life. *(Jangles a bell vigorously)* Ruthy Mae!

BUNKY. She hates that bell.

JASMINE. Oh God, another extension's slipping!

IRENE. *(Violently)* Ruthy Mae!

BUNKY. She's left for choir practice.

IRENE. I have no use for Ruthy Mae. She has a nursing degree, but it's such a waste. She just sings spirituals and wears that bandanna.

BUNKY. *(Exiting for the soup)* Why force-feed him?

IRENE. Sick people never want to eat. I was a volunteer—a candy striper at Mercy Hospital. *(Demandingly)* Jasmine!

JASMINE. *(Storms out, shrieking)* I can't feed him, when my hair's falling out.

IRENE. He'll eat, if he knows y'all want him to. *(Raises his pillow)* Well, Roo, your temperature's down.

BUNKY. I thought you said he looked bad...

IRENE. *(To **ROOSTER**)* Ruthy Mae made you some bouillon. It's made from the blood of baby cows. *(**ROOSTER** moans)* You boil the meat in water, then extract it to make this liquid with chunks of the richest beef. Rooster...Now take a few sips.

*(**ROOSTER** coughs and flails.)*

IRENE. Remember the airplane game you made Bunky play?

BUNKY. *(Making landing gestures with his hand)* The airplane is flying around—ready to land—one for Mimi, two for—Bunky.

ROOSTER. *(Flails his head away and coughs)* No. Not now!

BUNKY. Oh gosh, he's choking.

*(For the first time, **IRENE** knows in her marrow that **ROO** wants to die. She glares out at the estate, looming before her like a ghastly cemetery.)*

IRENE. Roo. I know I was against the preserve idea for Quint, but an artists' retreat for you might work. You could paint in the main house. And build cabins under those oak trees for your friends. I'll move back to town.

*(**IRENE** hovers over **ROO**, searching for the slightest twinkle in his eyes. **IRENE** lifts up his limp hand.)*

IRENE. Just squeeze my hand if you like the idea.

*(**ROOSTER**'s fingers fold down over **IRENE**'s jeweled hand.)*

IRENE. Fine, son. I had Clovis draw up this document, to transfer the rear property. *(Slips out a paper and a pen)* It's been witnessed, notarized, and now I'm signing it. Your only obligation is to be candid with me about what you do and for whom. *(Draws the net curtains about **ROO**'s bed)*

BUNKY. I wonder how Dad will take this.

IRENE. Shh! You're not going to tell him.

BUNKY. *(Exits inside, shaking his head)* He's a sophisticated investigator.

*(**LIGHTS**: As the sun sets, shadows stretch across the walls. Stripped of light, the gallery resembles a mausoleum.)*

IRENE. *(Calls sternly)* Jasmine! I plan to face many issues...that Quint's been knowing about. Jasmine, let's sit in the shadows. You used to be so good-looking. Now, whenever I come near you, there's only this scent.

JASMINE. It's Opium.

IRENE. *(Pulls out a box)* What would you call your hair color?

JASMINE. Ice brown.

IRENE. And your eyes?

JASMINE. China blue.

IRENE. My husband's Mississippi office just sent this to me. Pandora's fantasies.

*(**IRENE** casually opens a metal box and places a pistol on the table. She removes pictures.)*

IRENE. Photos of you and Pete...He had them all over his corporate apartment.

JASMINE. Our relationship was of no importance.

IRENE. *(Whisking up a gold-framed photo)* What's this of you two in bathrobes?

JASMINE. Old press shots.

IRENE. And these? *(Slips out videos and reads a box)* "Psycho sexual films with a spin."

JASMINE. You shouldn't concern yourself with that.

IRENE. *(Removes a paper)* And the insurance policy—leaving you ten million dollars?

JASMINE. I am legally his daughter.

IRENE. We're in redneck country. You can't go much further South.

JASMINE. I have my rights.

IRENE. There's no judge in this county going to give you a nickel.

JASMINE. I'm not like your limp-wristed children. I know where I'm going, so you can't cut my hands off.

IRENE. You think your little arrangement shocks me! Ha. I was married to Pete for forty years, and him to me for four, but not consecutively.

JASMINE. *(Her eyes drawn like a magnet to the silver pistol)* We never did it.

IRENE. *(She puts the gun away)* How much will it take for me never to see you again?

JASMINE. The insurance policy.

IRENE. Well…you'll have to subtract that from the money you owe me. *(Gestures casually to the stack of canceled checks)* DeBango's listed these checks drawn to you and the charges on our accounts, some ten point five million. He'll deduct that amount, with a fifteen percent interest over a ten-year period from any money willed you.

JASMINE. Oh, my God. Another clump of hair's falling out.

IRENE. Or shall we just call it even.

(IRENE rips the insurance policy in half.)

JASMINE. Oh my God! All these years, I thought of you as my mother.

IRENE. You should have put some savings aside.

JASMINE. I hoped one day you would love me, too.

IRENE. I've got to provide for my retirement.

JASMINE. Like when you built me that doll house. It blew down in that hurricane. But it was there. A miniature of yours with columns, a gallery, blue shutters. Inside I had your china dolls. No one else wanted them. The play furniture. I would rock for hours there, a princess in her castle, pretending she was you.

IRENE. Where was that house again?

JASMINE. On that slab. Near the grape arbor, yes. *(Shakes her head)* It's in my memory now, only in my memory.

(JASMINE rushes to the beach, and IRENE disappears inside. ROOSTER has overheard all. He pushes out of the mosquito netting, stares after IRENE and JASMINE. He picks up the deed, studies it. QUINT leaps on to the gallery. He has a bottle of champagne in one hand and crystal glasses in the other hand.)

QUINT. Rooster! Rooster! You feeling better? Champagne for the hospital report.

ROOSTER. *(Waves the deed)* Well, it worked! Grief made Mama generous.

QUINT. You're kidding. *(He fills the glasses)*

ROOSTER. This acting is a gas!

QUINT. Relax. You're still weak!

ROOSTER. Mama didn't allow for one character development—that you could rush me to town, and my shrink could glue me back together.

(ROOSTER presents the paper to **QUINT** *magisterially.* **QUINT** *skims the paper.)*

QUINT. All the rear property?

ROOSTER. Just a dot on the map of Mississippi. Now you can travel by yacht from here to New Orleans.

QUINT. Miles and miles of swamp land. You don't mean it?

ROOSTER. I'm trying to be as inextravagant with extravagances as possible. It's a process that involves vigilance and finesse.

QUINT. Roo, you shouldn't do this.

ROOSTER. I enjoyed being a boy here…fishing at dawn, hiking with a stick, launching paper boats. But some gifts have translucent strings.

QUINT. You're signing it over to me? Even the mineral rights?

*(***QUINT** *interrupts the euphoria of champagne and tobacco, and starts to dial the phone. He balances it with one ear, and refills his glass. He imitates the vocal quality of the Texan on the line.)*

QUINT. It's Quint speaking! Roy? Roy Rogers? The Lone Ranger. Well, are you still mounting Dale? I got the papers in my hand. Bring Silver on over. Let's get hitched. *(Hangs up)* Roy Fatswell. He never talks. You never know if he's a genius or a complete idiot.

IRENE. *(Enters)* Roo.

QUINT. *(Lifting the glass)* We got a good report at the hospital.

IRENE. You're not drinking my good champagne. I was saving that.

QUINT. Doctor Boudreau says Roo's been playing possum. Ha!

IRENE. Don't act foolish, Quint. Rooster Dubonnet, you get back to bed! I'm calling your doctor.

(IRENE dials the phone as **QUINT** *and* **ROOSTER** *giggle over champagne.* **BUNKY** *rushes into the room.* **BUNKY** *glances around for* **ROOSTER** *and seeing him, cries out.)*

BUNKY. God! Is Roo over-medicated? For God's sake, sit down.

IRENE. *(Idles the phone on her shoulder)* I'm a hostage of Gulf Coast Bell. Get my toddy, Bunky!

QUINT. How many times did you flunk out of school, son?

BUNKY. Four, Dad.

QUINT. This is loser's paradise. Jasmine's a "hand model"! Roo's a hypochondriac! And I'm a hack! Last week, I overdosed on Quaaludes, but Rooster kept me walking, walking, and talking!

ROOSTER. *(Waving his champagne)* We boys concocted this plan!

IRENE. *(Shouts into the phone)* I want Doctor Boudreau? Women doctors are harder than men, and she's the hardest woman doctor I know. What do you mean, she doesn't know what's going on? Rooster Dubonnet has gout! Ha! Gout!

QUINT. The disease of kings!

IRENE. Gout!

BUNKY. How could that doctor get the facts right and be so wrong!

IRENE. Let me speak to Dr. Boudreau. You sent her away! To silence her! *(The phone clicks off)*

*(**SOUND**: The phone rings.* **BUNKY** *picks it up.)*

BUNKY. *(Into the phone)* Hello? Who? Dad…It's a Mr. Fatswell. The one Mimi says sounds like a snake oil salesman.

QUINT. *(Bellows into the phone)* Roy! Hi-yo Silver! You want it? Well, you've got plenty of money. You've just got to turn it loose.

IRENE. Don't come to me when y'all overextend yourselves.

QUINT. No...Irene's thrilled with the refinery idea.

IRENE. *(Polishes her diamond against her skirt)* I don't have one note on any of my property.

QUINT. That tract in back, it's worth much more commercially.

IRENE. You're drunk with debt.

QUINT. *(Hangs up the phone)* No, drunk with life. I'm officially cutting the cord. Snip. I'm going to buy confidence with cash. Build dreams.

IRENE. *(Baiting him)* The bank must have approved another loan!

QUINT. Set the boys up in Tijuana. They won't have to pawn their youth for a little "blood money." *(Lifts his arms as if launching a ball)* I want y'all to live!

BUNKY. I've already lived! Now what do I do, Dad?

QUINT. Sunbathe on the Riviera. Scuba dive in Hawaii. Cruise to Greece! Life is for the beautiful and the young!

ROOSTER. *(Cheers as he heads offstage)* The signs of success! Yahoo! I'd better change. Yahoo!

QUINT. Well, let's get packed!

IRENE. You're one step ahead of the sheriff!

QUINT. Yep, you can't make a living in oil, but you can occasionally make a killing. Imagine yourself walking inside a portrait...this house and that Gulf. Underneath is a money machine spewing oil.

IRENE. Preposterous. Any oil would have gushed into the lines of our well.

QUINT. That's not what Roy Fatswell thinks. Yep! He wants to construct an oil complex. Storage tanks for holding. Housing for the workers.

IRENE. He's not going to ruin my land.

QUINT. Well, these acres and acres of currency don't really concern you!

*(**QUINT** slips **ROO**'s deed out of his pocket—unfolding it like a king unrolling a decree.)*

QUINT. You were Roo's chief beneficiary... Now I'm the one with deep pockets.

IRENE. You want to play hardball? I'm on the board of every bank in Mississippi.

QUINT. I know, Mrs. Dubonnet. But Roo's given the rear land to me. And I've sold it to the snake oil salesman.

IRENE. Oil field trash! It's greed like yours that's polluting the South. Nature's screaming and you're going to pay.

QUINT. This oil company's donating fifty million dollars to preserve sea life—going extinct.

IRENE. You can't turn the sacred into the profane that easy. There is that bill.

QUINT. Which will be reversed. Go get packed, son.

IRENE. Claw your way to the top, and you'll get nowhere. My family owns this town.

QUINT. No one cares about your ancestry. It's whether or not this deal's lucrative. The bad boys are in politics. It's a gangster's business, not a gentleman's profession. The South is driven by greed, by little bitty politicians with little bitty men's hang-ups. They'll take my money.

IRENE. Bribery!

QUINT. Ignorance! Without politics for a living, most of them would raise dogs!

*(A fog horn booms. **QUINT** rushes down the stairs— revitalized by the sounds coming from the yacht. He squints out over the lawn, flicks the gallery lights, and bellows, "Ship Ahoy!" **BUNKY** peers through **JASMINE**'s telescope as **IRENE** walks to the edge of the gallery. **JASMINE**, at an upstage window, her eyes swollen with tears, observes the events.)*

BUNKY. There's a tremendous ship gleaming under the moon. Looks like a space ship!

QUINT. That yacht's my ticket out of this hell hole. Bunky, start packing for Florida.

IRENE. Florida isn't even the South. It's lower Manhattan. We'll discuss this in the morning, Quint.

QUINT. At dawn, I'll be off on that yacht. Fatswell's taking the President of Hancock Bank in Gulfport and the Whitney in New Orleans to a...very rich lunch...you get my picture. He's going to be handing out a lot more than food.

IRENE. That's illegal.

QUINT. That's Louisiana! Are you ready, son?

IRENE. *(Presses her hand over her chest)* Bunky, my heart pills are in my tan purse.

BUNKY. *(Running for the pills)* She's been pacing up and down all day, Dad!

*(**LIGHTS**: The gallery glows with the warmth of the gold moon.)*

*(**JASMINE** enters.)*

QUINT. Did you get your insurance pledge?

JASMINE. I let her burn it up. You're dallying with danger, Quint. I overheard.

QUINT. So? Just put on my tombstone, "He was fearless."

JASMINE. Irene Dubonnet's all the family I've known.

QUINT. Family!

JASMINE. I told you. I didn't do it...

QUINT. Just above the waist. I've reserved the use of the entire grounds twice a year for entertaining.

JASMINE. Who wants to party around an oil rig?

QUINT. Me.

JASMINE. You have this callousness that's quite seductive.

*(**JASMINE** strolls down front to hear the crickets and the rush of the Gulf water. **JASMINE** breathes in the salty air. For the first time, she realizes she won't see Pete Dubonnet again. Modern technology—mud, wires, and metal braces—will replace her memories. **QUINT**'s hand touches **JASMINE**'s shoulder.)*

QUINT. It's not yours, sugar. No one gave the land to you.

JASMINE. God, you're uncouth!

QUINT. This place was meant for the family sons. It dropped into my lap like a dead leaf, because the last uptown prince didn't care.

JASMINE. Irene Dubonnet's greedy but she's...refined.

QUINT. The plantation mentality. "Debutante-ti-tis." No one schooled your people to put back. They were raised to think that they were owed service by birthright. Fool notion's been bulldozed into their heads.

(SOUND: Horn.)

JASMINE. I'm not ready to gloss this over with a deluxe cruise, with yet another hustle to erase the past. Screwing your family has repercussions.

QUINT. Life has repercussions. It's the start of the new South, of a more democratic way of doing business. Once the news of oil hits the street, these mansions will be nothing but shells. That's reality, honey.

(SOUND: Once again there is a signal from the yacht.)

QUINT. *(Wrapping his arm around her shoulder)* Let's go.

JASMINE. I've no clothes packed.

QUINT. For the daytime, I'll buy you a trousseau from Paris.

JASMINE. And for the nighttime?

QUINT. *(Pressing her hair back behind her ear)* Nothing. I want to marry you, Jazz.

JASMINE. Me too. My enemies are going to drool. They drooled over your Jaguar and now they'll drool over our yacht.

QUINT. God, I love to make you happy!

JASMINE. Buy me a big diamond, will you, Quint? A solitaire. What's the largest they make? Twenty carats?

QUINT. Yeah. You'll sail past forty with more diamonds than Elizabeth Taylor.

(**QUINT** *puts his arm around her, and they saunter out the front gallery.* **QUINT** *yells back.)*

QUINT. Rooster, boy. We're sending someone back for you.

JASMINE. So much of everything, so little of nothing!

QUINT. Don't look back!

(**IRENE** *and* **BUNKY** *enter and hear tires crushing the oyster shells.)*

IRENE. There they go—running on quicksand. I haven't a single trump card except privilege. They're spoilt, so they'll be back.

BUNKY. A temporary star. Temporary stars destroy themselves in one explosion...

ROOSTER. *(Enters humming, sporting a cane with a silver pelican head)* Kierkegaard said, "Don't finish with life, until life is finished with you."

IRENE. You're such a ham actor. You should join the St. Louis Cathedral Drama Society.

ROOSTER. I'd rather recuperate with a nurse on that yacht. It'll be hectic but fun...like sipping water from a fire hydrant! Water my plants! Chase the ducks! And feed Boon. Can't forget him! You ready, Bunky?

BUNKY. No.

*(**SOUND**: The walls rattle as Phantom runs off.)*

BUNKY. Phantom's run off. He was playing possum, too!

ROOSTER. Bye, Irene! *(Goes to kiss her but she raises her hand to stop him)*

IRENE. All animals can think. What sets humans apart is our ability to deceive ourselves.

ROOSTER. *(Blows her a kiss)* I'll send you a sketch.

(BUNKY crosses and feeds the goldfish.)

BUNKY. Goldfish will eat until they burst.

IRENE. *(Opens some shutters to reveal a splendid cake.)* It was supposed to be a surprise birthday but everyone's left. When home life is bad, people take it out on the person in charge.

BUNKY. I can't eat.

IRENE. Go on!

BUNKY. Remember when I went away to St. Paul's Boarding School. You wrote me twice a day...with a program for my career.

IRENE. You returned the letters—stamped "addressee unknown." I knew you were alive because you kept cashing checks. It's not me you love, it's my function!

BUNKY. After Mama left, I wrote.

IRENE. *(Glancing in a mirror, touches her cheekbones)* Men of the South, if they have white hair, people say they're so distinguished. A woman with the same hair, they say she should color it.

BUNKY. Will you listen to me! *(Rocking back and forth on a chair)* I might as well dive into a tank of sharks.

IRENE. Don't do that! You're going to fall on your face.

BUNKY. Like Houdini, just tie me inside a box and toss me in the Gulf. I'll get out. I'm living in the gray zone...I have to hurt myself to get attention.

(BUNKY raises his arms theatrically, acting out various circus acts.)

BUNKY. Blindfold myself for the high wires! Race a cycle down a silver cord! Flip from one trapeze to the next with a sword in my teeth!

IRENE. I ordered you an Arabian stallion. It's all white.

BUNKY. Give him to Clarence. *(He pulls out a silver gun)*

IRENE. Where did you get that?

BUNKY. In the box—next to the photos. Everyone has one!

IRENE. Put it back.

(BUNKY stretches his arm in the air like a trained marksman and points at three spots over the Gulf.)

BUNKY. Here's to Dad, to Jasmine, and to Roo.

IRENE. Give it here!

BUNKY. Our home life is a nightmare. There's this machine—*(Gestures with the gun)*—that needs feeding, and a staff that's overworked! People are so trapped in their own panic that no one notices anyone else.

IRENE. Hand me the gun.

BUNKY. Don't tell me how to act! *(Squeezing his hand over the gun)*

IRENE. What's wrong, son?

BUNKY. I have this anguish inside me. I don't know where it's coming from.

IRENE. Life!

BUNKY. *(Stroking the barrel with his finger)* I've been dreaming about Mama. It's funny, but I can never recall Mama holding me as a child.

IRENE. That's Southerners! We miss the people we hate.

BUNKY. And now it's August.

(BUNKY takes the gun and strolls to the edge of the gallery.)

BUNKY. At midnight, I'll be twenty-one!

IRENE. *(Never taking her eyes off the gun)* You don't want the horse, we'll return it. This is the most important birthday of your life.

BUNKY. *(Stares at the water, the salt air bites his cheeks)* No one's here.

IRENE. We'll celebrate again next week. Make a list of your friends.

BUNKY. Sure. I feel like a jellyfish on the beach. I'm flopping around with no direction. There's this Cajun restaurant near Mama that needs waiters. I could work there and sleep at a youth hostel.

IRENE. You don't know anything about..."hostels"! You're not going to go out hawking yourself.

BUNKY. Thought I'd hitchhike across the U.S. and then go overseas.

IRENE. What will you do?

BUNKY. Experiment. Living to a formula prevents chances that might happen along the way. Maybe I'll join the Marines. I've got so much despair inside, it'll take boot camp to get it out. I'm spending the night at the Gulf Shores Hotel.

IRENE. People go there to live out their fantasies...from the ridiculous to the sublime.

BUNKY. I want to go to dangerous places, where I have to defend ideas that feel right...even if I can't express them. You'll never be far from me.

IRENE. I'm sixty-plus, son. I'm old South. We come on this earth for a short time when you consider all the centuries. We make a little tour and we're gone.

BUNKY. I won't drop out of sight.

IRENE. Stay the night!

BUNKY. I can't. There's this old rage creeping inside me...I can't shake it because I trusted the wrong people. My family! People who raised me, who I thought were right...Y'all told me stories about life that aren't true. Misrepresentations! Nothing matters here unless it can be measured in money.

(BUNKY *begins checking the barrel of the gun. It shines like a diamond in the moonlight.)*

IRENE. For God's sake, will you put that up? You expect too much. You're just a student. The only duty of a student is to...

BUNKY. Learn well...I don't know how to gauge myself...Everyone's gone and left me with these lies.

(BUNKY *rushes off stage.)*

(LIGHTS: *The moonlight streams in, glistening like glass across the cold floor.)*

(IRENE *dashes for the phone.)*

IRENE. *(Screaming offstage)* I'm still here.

(BUNKY *reenters, putting on his backpack. He slams down her phone.)*

BUNKY. There's too much of you inside and not enough of me. It's emotional plagiarism!

IRENE. It's not a question of plagiarism. We're all appropriating each other.

BUNKY. Since Grandpa's death, I've been copying your rules, and they're shackling. I figure I'd better develop my own smoke alarm. I'm not stable inside. If I don't leave, Mimi, I'll be headed for trouble.

IRENE. I've been counting on you to lead this family. You're our bright star! *(Removes a money clip)* Throw away money. Buy whatever you want! Talent doesn't pass from father to son, but money does.

BUNKY. No, thanks.

IRENE. The rewards here are fiduciary, not emotional. Grandpa's left you and Rooster everything...if you finish your studies.

BUNKY. If? What about Jasmine and Mama?

IRENE. Girls don't count. Same thing happened to me! *(Pressing the money at him)* Take this.

BUNKY. No! *(Puts the gun in his pocket)* Nothing! My favorite stimulus is panic. *(He laughs)* Da! Da!

IRENE. It'd make me happier if you'd leave the gun.

BUNKY. I'm not going to stop loving you because I'm away.

IRENE. Switch on the lights before you go. Flick the air conditioner on "super cool."

BUNKY. I thought you were saving money.

IRENE. For what?

*(**LIGHTS**: The lights flick on behind **IRENE**, illuminating the mansion like a giant mausoleum. The air conditioner bumps on, and the door slams. The yard lights flash on. **IRENE** flips cards—occasionally she blots her eyes with a lace handkerchief, sniffs and runs her tongue over her teeth. A calliope from the church fair plays in the distance.)*

*(**IRENE** addresses the audience.)*

IRENE. I belong to a breed of Southern women—now going extinct—who dedicate their lives to finding rich husbands and having sons. Harmony that's all I'm after...peace in the family. Dissension jeopardizes the simplest things: a lovely dinner, a quiet afternoon, an evening stroll. What is life but a chain of little pleasures? Breakfast in bed, fresh cut flowers, a steam and a Swiss massage...

*(**SOUND**: Something like Jacques Brel music plays.)*

IRENE. French cabaret music, your grandson's smile, fireworks on the Fourth of July...We have anything you'd want on the Gulf Coast. Passion for us is having an affair with your eyes. Where else can you grow such glorious hydrangeas and hear a calliope from the church fair? My house only looks good when there are a hundred people inside. I wouldn't live any place you couldn't hear the waves lapping the beach, see the shadows from the oak trees, where it's never too early or too late to have mint juleps on the veranda. *(Flips a card)* The red suit looks good. *(Turns a queen card)* The Queen of Diamonds! Sometimes the queen must go into her tower and cry. All great queens do. And sometimes she must say, "Off with their heads."

*(**LIGHTS**: Blackout.)*

*(**SOUND**: Blues music comes up for the)*

(curtain)

Also by
Rosary Hartel O'Neill...

The Awakening of Kate Chopin

Black Jack: The Thief of Possession

Degas in New Orleans

John Singer Sargent and Madame X

Marilyn/God

Property

Solitaire

Turtle Soup

Uncle Victor

White Suits in Summer

The Wings of Madness

Wishing Aces

Please visit our website **samuelfrench.com** for complete descriptions and licensing information.

OTHER TITLES AVAILABLE FROM SAMUEL FRENCH

PROPERTY

Rosary Hartel O'Neill

Full Length, Southern Comedy / 2m, 3f / Unit set

Property is a contemporary romantic comedy set in a Garden District mansion in New Orleans. Rooster Dubonnet, a young artist suffering from a terminal disease, is dazzled by love. Raised by an imperious society-driven mother, he has fallen in love with a New-Age nurse. Set during Mardi Gras–when a whole tradition of fun, revelry, and prestige seizes the city– Rooster is caught between his dedication to his family's past (and "property") and his own very different future.

OTHER TITLES AVAILABLE FROM SAMUEL FRENCH

THE AWAKENING OF KATE CHOPIN

Rosary Hartel O'Neill

Full Length, Historical Drama / 2m, 2f

Kate Chopin, author of *The Awakening*, struggles to hold onto her marriage and her six small children as she launches her career as a novelist in 1884. Frustrating her attempts are: her wealthy next door neighbor, wanting to prove his masculinity; her jealous husband, stricken with malaria; the little sex-pot seamstress next door, the town gossip; and the bankrupt cotton business, which consumes all of her time. This crazy cacophony of personalities ends up compelling Kate toward her goal of becoming a famous author.

SAMUELFRENCH.COM

OTHER TITLES AVAILABLE FROM SAMUEL FRENCH

DEGAS IN NEW ORLEANS

Rosary Hartel O'Neill

Full Length, Drama / 3m, 6f / One integrated int/ext set.

A historical drama that explores Edgar Degas' scandalous visit to New Orleans in 1872. Edgar Degas, the French Impressionist painter, is torn between helping his relatives in America and pursuing a career as a painter. Fame and family obligations come to a head when he discovers he is still in love with his sister-in-law, who is now pregnant and blind. As Edgar struggles with his own ethical conundrum, he discovers that his aggressively charming brother has gone through all the family money in an attempt to save his uncle's sugar business.

SAMUELFRENCH.COM

OTHER TITLES AVAILABLE FROM SAMUEL FRENCH

WHITE SUITS IN SUMMER

Rosary Hartel O'Neill

Full Length, Comedy / 2m, 2f / Unit Set

This contemporary Southern romance set in the topsy-turvy world of art. Celebrity artist Susann is determined to reclaim her lost love, Blaise, now married to a sedate New Orleans socialite. Convinced that she cannot live without him, Susann arranges an exhibition of her works to be held in his new house. Susann's readiness to sacrifice her career, his new wife, and her Mama's boy manager leave Blaise both angry and aroused. Theatrical excitement abounds in this comedy of love vs. duty.

SAMUELFRENCH.COM

www.ingramcontent.com/pod-product-compliance
Lightning Source LLC
Chambersburg PA
CBHW070650300426
44111CB00013B/2350